Work From Home

How To Find The Best Jobs

By Joe Brown

2020

Summary

Technology has made it possible for companies to adopt the approach of allowing some or the entire employee to work from home. Apart from helping these companies to reduce operational costs, it has the potential to increase productivity. How can you be more productive and successful when working from home? Worry no more! From this guide, you'll get all the crucial information about work from home. This includes critical information about the primary sources of work from home job posts and top-rated categories of homeworking jobs. Also, you will know the essential things to note about working from home, and how you can be more productive and successful. Let's get started!

Work From Home

Summary

Introduction

Chapter 1: Sources Of Homeworking Jobs

Health And Medical Sector

Education

Government

Technology And Engineering

Chapter 2: Friendly Companies Offering Work From Home Jobs

AMZN

Dell Inc.

Humana Inc.

Aetna Inc.

American Express Co.

Kaplan

Salesforce.com Inc

Automatic Data Processing

IBM

Xerox Corp

Chapter 3: Top-Rated Categories Of Homeworking Jobs

Virtual Assistant

Translators

Customer Service Representatives

Transcription And Data Entry

Tutor

Take Note Of The Scams

Chapter 4: Crucial Things To Note About Homeworking Jobs

1.   You Determine Your Success or Failure

2. Meet Deadlines

3. It's Impossible To Leave The Office

4. It May Be Hard To Save

Chapter 5: How To Get The Most Out Of Homeworking

1.   Come Up With A Schedule

2. Batch What You're Doing

3. Dress In The Morning

4. Always Stop A Specific Time

5. Set Aside Some Days For Meetings And Other Tasks

6. Track All Hours

7. Create A Boundary Between 'Home' Space And 'Work' Space

8. Decluttering The Physical Space

9. Purchase Ergonomic and Comfortable Furniture To Use In Your Office

10. The Right Ambiance

11. Avoid Social Media

12. Check Emails At Specific Times

13. Set Expectations About Working Time

14. Productive Ways For Procrastinating

15. As For Help If You're A Parent

16. Turn Off Notifications

17. Use The Most Appropriate Tools To Remain On Track

18. Noise-Canceling Headphones

19. Online Community

20. Leave Your House

21. Keep Friends And Family Members Informed About Your Work

22. Break The Routine At Least Once In A While

23. 20-20-20 Rule

Conclusion

References

Introduction

Nowadays, work from home is a day-to-day term in every place. Most people are now shifting their attention from working from home towards homeworking. The technologies which keep changing from one day to another have contributed heavily to the rapid expansion of the homeworking taskforce. Examples of these technologies include cloud computing, Skype, Authenticator applications, Slack, and Facetime. Also, with the help of email and texting, you don't need to work from office so that you can get classified as a productive member. The fact is that you can successfully and effectively complete a significant percentage of the jobs from your home office.

Just like remote work, the homeworking job force also comes with several outstanding benefits. All these have made most companies implement virtual workplaces. These organizations have done so since virtual workplaces save a lot when it comes to office facilities. Research shows that with these virtual workplaces, companies are likely to save up to 10,000 US dollars per employee for one year.

With virtual workplaces, companies will create an excellent environment for higher employee productivity. Also, virtual workplaces are the most preferred because they record fewer cases of missed workdays as a result of commuting problems or sickness. Other than this, virtual workplaces allow companies to enjoy access to many potential workers from whom they will choose the best ones. Also, a distributed job force helps a lot whenever a manmade or natural-related disaster occurs. When these happen, the organization will still continue to run as usual, even in cases where some employees go offline.

Chapter 1: Sources Of Homeworking Jobs

The exciting thing to note is that homeworking jobs are now diversified. They are not restricted to multi-level marketing outfits such as Avon. Most businesses have now started offering homeworking jobs because of improved technology. Also, these companies have opted for homeworking because they want to cut their costs and save more. Examples of sources of homeworking jobs are:

Health And Medical Sector

This sector features many many companies offering homeworking jobs. Examples of the top-rated ones include UnitedHealth Group, Humana, Covance, Aetna, Paraxel, Forest Laboratories, and many more. Some of the homeworking jobs they offer include phone-based and computer-based ones, and they include sales representatives, business-intelligence managers, medical writers, patient-case advocates, and patient-education advocates. Others include revenue-integrity directors, account managers, actuarial consultants, and case managers. The recent remote jobs offered by these companies include registered nurse case managers and clinical nurse case managers.

Education

Education is a field that most people cannot accept if it offers work from home tasks. However, online learning has led to the introduction of work from home jobs in this field. Some of the companies offering online education include Tutor.com, InstaEDU, Connections Academy, and many more. These companies are behind the establishment of part-time tasks and freelance positions such as parent mentors, curriculum writers, and SAT instructors. Other homeworking jobs include parent mentors, student-services coordinators, and science teachers. Also, there is VIPKID, which is an online education company in China, exposing the young-aged Chinese students to American education. Furthermore, this education firm offers a flexible, homeworking plan for its online-teaching workforce.

Other excellent opportunities in this field are for those who are fluent in various languages. It is in this niche that we come across firms such as Appen, which play a crucial role in evaluating and coordinating communications for clients from all parts of the world. Also, there is Asurion, which is the best for offering customer support in different languages for electronics firms' product insurance plans. These companies need the help of translators and interpreters.

Government

You cannot immediately associate Government agencies with unconventional or innovative related personnel policies. However, some of the national-level, state-level, and local-level institutions have now adopted the flexible types of works. For example, the federal government has been at the forefront of promoting telecommuting in the last few years. In fact, the federal government leads private companies when it comes to instilling telecommuting policies.

Also, the federal government leads these firms by educating the employees on the benefits of working from home. Research shows that out of three federal government employees, one of them works from home at a particular moment during the year. The agencies led by the federal government include the department in charge of Transportation, the department in charge of agriculture, and the department in charge of the interior. Some of the homeworking jobs, in this case, include emergency services planners, security specialists, economic assistants, and affairs officers.

Technology And Engineering

A surprising fact is that the friendly categories of homeworking are technology. Also, technology is one thing that has led to the establishment of engineering and virtual offices, and they usually offer these services in the form of a per-project basis. Some of the top-rated employers in this sector include SAP, IBM, RedHat, and First Data. Also, most of the homeworking jobs offered by these companies are high-tech sales. Other than this, remote workers can get jobs like technical writers, software developers, project managers, power-system engineers, and web-designers.

Chapter 2: Friendly Companies Offering Work From Home Jobs

The majority of the legit firms, even the ones under the Fortune 500, provide many telecommuting job opportunities. These tasks include the positions that require experienced individuals, those with advanced degrees, and even those with entry-level gigs. Some of the top-rated corporations to consider for an excellent homeworking job include:

AMZN

Amazon.com Inc. has employed over 500,000 employees, and all these come from different parts of the world. Most of these workers perform their roles from offices situated in their homes. It is only a few employees who work in the firm's headquarters, located in Washington state. The company has spread all its employees to all parts of the world. Also, all these employees love their roles and are not ready to reassign.

Dell Inc.

Dell is another top-rated firm offering friendly work from home jobs, and its headquarters are situated in Austin, Texas. Other than homeworking jobs, Dell also offers flexible tasks such as working remotely and office time. Also, this company is the most popular for its many more worker-friendly perks like compressed workweeks. Dell offers homeworking jobs in several fields, and the experience and education levels required vary from one to another. These positions range all the way from marketing management and tech support up to outside sales.

Humana Inc.

Human Inc. is a health insurance firm that has over 50,000 employees, and all these work from their home offices and on-site. Those working from their home offices do every task from sales management, a position that demands basic educational requirements, up to physical therapy, a job post that requires post-college coursework experience.

Aetna Inc.

With Aetna Inc., you can decide to work from your home office after you've worked with this firm for a year. The telecommuting positions offered by this company include frontline nurses, customer service representatives, and supervisors. With this company, when you work from your home office, you will enjoy the freedom of accessing extensive technology. Through this, you will get updated from time to time about the progress of the firm and maintain excellent communication with your workmates.

American Express Co.

American Express Co. is another top-rated firm offering friendly homeworking jobs. With this company, you will have access to contract, full-time, and even part-time homeworking jobs. The company provides a variety of homeworking jobs that cover several opportunities, such as business development and part-time customer service. Other than this, Americal Express is one of the top-rated companies that encourage personal growth and a great work-life balance for their employees.

Kaplan

Kaplan refers to the tutoring firm that helps those students preparing for the standardized tests needed so that they get admitted to graduate schools or colleges. Tutoring is the most popular homeworking job that this tutoring company offers. Yes, the position many need no or little office time, but you may be required to travel to meet your students.

Kaplan pays its tutors $20 or more per hour, and they can work up to 40 hours per week, but this depends on the demand for the service and their availability. Also, this firm hires only candidates who demonstrate high performance on standardized tests.

Salesforce.com Inc

Fortune Magazine categorized Salesforce.com under the top-rated firms to work for. Also, *Forbes* named Saleforce.com under the category of the most innovative firms in the world. It is one of the most rated firms offering friendly work from home jobs with over 25,000 of its employees working from home. However, the telecommuting job positions offered by this company demands several years of experience. The work from home tasks for entry-level candidates includes sales jobs like field sales account executives.

Automatic Data Processing

Automatic Data Processing helps businesses from different parts of the world when it comes to the provision of payroll and outsourcing-related solutions. The most popular homeworking jobs it offers include customer support and sales service. Thus, this shows that there is a high probability for an entry-level candidate to get a job. Other works from home tasks offered by this firm include application and software development, but this demands specialized technology skills.

IBM

With IBM, candidates in the US or from other parts of the world can get a telecommuting job. Other than this, the International Business Machines company is the perfect place for freelances looking for homeworking jobs. It hires researches, software developers, and chemists who wish to work on contract projects and receive payment by post. Also, most of those working with IBM can work from their home offices. An exciting benefit with freelance jobs is that most of them are after a unique skill and not work background or a specific degree.

Xerox Corp

Xerox Corp is also the perfect option if you're looking for a friendly work from home job. Other than this, this is the most preferred firm by many employees because it offers since it provides flexible scheduling for the majority of those working on-site. The most common work from home tasks provided by this company includes project management, a position that several years of experience in this field, and call center position, which don't demand educational background. Another telecommuting job offered by this company is executive recruiting, and this requires sales experience and a bachelor's degree.

Chapter 3: Top-Rated Categories Of Homeworking Jobs

Not every homeworking job post is for a corporate employee. The majority of the individuals work for companies as freelancers, where they choose to come up with their own businesses. Also, as said earlier, many firms are now positioning their attentions to independent contractors so that they can fill several positions. Homeworking is also the perfect option for those with organizational skills, time, and capable of managing two to three projects simultaneously. Most of the enterprise types end up turning up freelance homeworking jobs into a small business and even employing some of these workers.

Below are excellent examples of top-rated categories of homeworking jobs. Some of these positions demand specialized expertise and training, as others don't require an educational background or experience.

Virtual Assistant

A virtual assistant is an employee whom you can compare with an off-site secretary. For the case of a traditional secretary, a company is likely to spend a lot. Also, for a small company, there is no need to hire a full-time secretary. For virtual assistants, they work from their home offices, and they communicate with their bosses via Slack, chat, or any other real-time service.

The exciting/peculiar characteristic of these employees is that they can handle any task that a traditional secretary can do. These tasks include data entry, calling clients, managing social media, scheduling appointments, creating company documents, booking, and responding to different emails. Also, virtual assistants are the most preferred because they can do all these at a lower cost. The primary talents needed for this job post include some little office experience and excellent communication skills.

Translators

When it comes to the case of international companies, they always need translators from time to time. Here, translators help in transcribing and translating conference calls and conversations or translating documents and files. Those speaking different languages have a higher demand, and the current has several home-based positions in this field.

Customer Service Representatives

Currently, most organizations, both small and large, are outsourcing their customer support service tasks to agents working from home offices. They do this since customers are likely to have issues while communicating with agents who are not native English speakers or those with heavy accents. Thus, that's why most developed companies are after more customer service representatives who are in the US.

The majority of the jobs for customer service representatives involve inbound calls, where they help people with account information or orders. Also, others entail outbound calling. Other than this, several others involve a set work schedule, but companies pay in the form of hours or per minute. In this case, organizations hire individuals who possess people skills and excellent communication skills. Also, most companies will go further into background checks when recruiting customer service representatives. Mostly, companies hire traditional customer service representatives to answer the questions of the

customers, live through social media, or the
website of the firm.

Transcription And Data Entry

Yes, jobs vary from one another, but transcription
tasks and data entry are two types of job posts that
demand similar qualifications and skills. In the
case of data entry, it entails filling a spreadsheet or
software program with facts and figures. Here, a
firm hires you to work hand-in-hand with a
customer management system and enter inventory
items, catalog items, or payroll data.

For the case of transcription, the home-based
worker creates documents from different audio
files. This work is primarily meant for those
companies that need a podcast, conference calls,
workshops, or meeting docs. Mostly, the company
will give the content management system and
software required for the task. When recruiting the
workers, the company will hire detail-oriented and
those individuals with excellent typing skills.

Tutor

Currently, online instructors are hotcakes because
of the development of online education. A virtual
school is a collective term everywhere. These
schools specialize in offering college-level study
programs and high school-level study programs.
Also, the exciting thing to note is that the faculty
of these schools can work from any place.

Yes, most online teaching job posts need teaching
credentials, but online tutoring does not need this.
However, the company will always check the
tutors' educational background before recruiting
them. In this field, you're likely to earn higher
hourly rates if you do online tutoring for advanced
subjects like physics and calculus. Also, you're
likely to come across an opportunity of doing

standardized test scoring directly from your home. For the case of scoring tasks, they may need a college degree or teaching background.

Take Note Of The Scams

Homeworking started from those money-making ads, but now we're talking of a new story. However, research still shows that every legitimate gig comes with an average of 57 scams. Therefore, being extra careful is the right stuff to do if you plan to work from home.
It is crucial to take your time, get more information about the homeworking employer before you decide to work with it. Always consider working with an established company. The best and trustable company must have evidence that it sells a particular product, and it possesses a physical address. Also, don't forget to check the contact information of the company and confirm if it's working. Note that the current web is full of con artists who pretend to be workers for corporations.

Remember that the best job must demand an application and even an interview. The best and trustable employer must be willing to meet or talk to you before they recruit you. Finally, don't pay to get a homeworking job. Therefore, you should always consider any homeworking opportunity as a scam if it requires you to pay. However, be ready to invest some money so that you can have a fast internet connection that you can rely on. You only need to do this if you don't have one.

Chapter 4: Crucial Things To Note About Homeworking Jobs

Just like office works, homeworking jobs come with merits and demerits. However, the advantages of homeworking are more compared to its disadvantages, meaning it is still the best option to go for. Other than this, there are some crucial tips you need to note so that you can make the most from homeworking. These include:

1. You Determine Your Success or Failure

When working from your home office, you have the option of determining the amount of work you can complete. Thus, this is a clear sign that success or failure is on your hands. The ability to hustle, concentrate, or interact with others is up to you. Also, what you produce and receive is up to you. Therefore, no day you will find yourself blaming because of your unproductive workday since you're the one in your home office.

You'll still remain to be your own boss even in cases where you work as a virtual assistant. So, be ready to get lonely and face the same things from one day to another if you choose to work from your home office.

2. Meet Deadlines

Be prepared to deal with individuals who don't categorize homeworking as a job. So, you need to decide on the best hours to work and stick to them. Don't allow anyone to interrupt you when following your work schedule. Don't let others see you as an employed individual since they will end up interfering with your schedule, something which will affect you at the end of the day. However, you need to note that home life comes with its own distractions. These are likely to interfere with your work schedule and put you behind on crucial projects. Some of the typical interruptions include child needs, animal needs, accidents, vendor calls, or power outages. Other than this, there are many more personal boundaries that are likely to interfere with your schedule.

Let your family members understand that it's impossible to help them move when working. Also, let them know that it is impossible to chat on the phone while working. Sometimes it can be hard to set limits if you're a parent. Also, the positive side is that you're likely to affect the future attitudes of your children and career choices when they see you working extra hard on the field you love.

3. It's Impossible To Leave The Office

Most people prefer working from home primarily because of flexibility and efficiency. Also, shorter hours make many individuals opt for homeworking. With homeworking, you enjoy completing your daily hours working on the assigned task without getting interrupted by staff meetings or emails. However, sometimes it's impossible to treat your home as an office. Also, you may find it hard to pretend you're working away from your home.

Mostly, the majority of home-based workers end up working more hours because of poor time management. Also, others will end up logging in their work time on weekends or nights because they never followed their schedule.

Research shows that most home-based employees work for five hours a day instead of eight hours. However, this does not indicate that they don't complete the daily tasks. Companies calculate hours as billable hours, which means that every hour they charge for, many minutes are spent on the non-compensated tasks.

4. It May Be Hard To Save

You may think that work from home will boost your budget because there is no cost for office attire, mandatory lunches, or daily commute, but that's wrong. There are many more costs that are likely to crop up. To set up an office, you need business services, cell phones, laptops, software, web hosting, internet service, printers, and business cards. Therefore, keeping all these in mind is the right stuff to do before choosing work from home.

Be prepared to deduct half of your mortgage to cover the expensed of the internet or your home office. Also, homeworking comes with strict limits on what you can claim as return credits or return deductions. You will have the option of deducting valid work expenses, but only from what you for your work. Thus, this means it's impossible to deduct the entire cost if you make payments for the internet service that you, your children, and spouse use for matters not related to your work. You only need to deduct the portion that is meant primarily on issues relating to employment. Do the same thing for office utilities, office telephone bills, and office supplies.

For independent contractors, you need to make payments for your payroll taxes, which is expensed that most workers pay for and Social Security tax- which is the self-employment tax. Therefore, homeworking won't record drastic cuts when it comes to tax bills.

Chapter 5: How To Get The Most Out Of Homeworking

Research shows that around four million individuals work from home. Other than this, managers from different companies say that home-based employees are more productive compared to office-employees.

Other than being more efficient, home-based workers report fewer cases of stress. This positive record is what leads to lower absenteeism and higher morale. Also, homeworking is the perfect choice for the environment, organizations, and even employees.

However, work from home also comes with its own issues. These range from job and professional challenges to physical and mental problems. So, which path can you follow to become more productive and remain healthy at the same time? Here is the answer:

1. Come Up With A Schedule

The majority of people prefer working from home because it allows them to come with their own schedules. It guarantees you the freedom to do what you like at any time. You only have a few hours to work and then spend the remaining time doing something that pleases your mind.

However, being careful not to end up wasting the whole day should be your first priority. Come up with the most favorable routine as per your needs so that you can always accomplish something worth it each day.

Eating your meals at specific times of the day is the best thing to do when working from home. Also, you need to start your work and put a full stop at the same time every day of the week.

With an excellent schedule, you will know when to work and when to go for a break, attend a meeting or call someone.

2. Batch What You're Doing

Yes, a work schedule can help a lot in achieving your daily goals, but it is also crucial to batch your daily tasks. By doing this, you will end up doing more work within the shortest possible.
As the latest research, multitasking is not the right path to follow since it makes us less productive. Therefore, batching work should remain to be the perfect option if you to be more productive and successful.

When you batch what you need to do, you will have the work done correctly within the shortest possible and as required. For example, if you prepare your meal schedule for the whole week on Monday, you will end up saving more time. Another excellent example is to set aside one month and plan everything you will post on your social media platforms for the remaining months. You will realize this is a fantastic step since it will save much of your time and money.

3. Dress In The Morning

Most individuals will always find it hassle-free to wake up from their beds and go directly to their home office. Yes, it is a productive step to take, but there is something you need to do to make it even more successful.

When you put on real clothes before starting to work, you prepare your mind to focus entirely on the day's workforce. Other than this, there is a high probability of becoming more productive when you work while wearing your real clothes. So, don't work while wearing your sweatpants. As per research, the level of our success and thoughts are affected by what we wear.

4. Always Stop A Specific Time

You can only keep your schedule if you start the project and stop at the specified time. You're likely to become lazy and say you have more time when working from home. Ths case also happens when you work from an office and plan to quite at a specific time.

However, you can become productive and successful only if you decide to follow your daily schedule. There is a high probability of quitting your job if you always struggle to stop work.

You're likely to interrupt your work by deciding to have a happy moment with your colleagues. Also, you will experience this if you choose to enjoy dinner with your family members and many more. You're not productive or successful if you always work more than eight hours per day. When you work for exactly eight hours, you give your mind and body enough time to relax and refresh.

5. Set Aside Some Days For Meetings And Other Tasks

You can only meet your daily schedules if you set aside some days for calls, or any other task not related to your day-to-day project. When you do this, you will prepare your mind well for that day so that you can become more active.

Other than this, when you set aside some days for calls and meetings, you will minimize interruptions, meaning you will focus more on the day-to-day tasks. Also, setting aside some days for meetings and other tasks will give you the peace of mind you need.

6. Track All Hours

It is crucial to track all your hours so that you can get a clear picture of how you always spend your time. Yes, you may be monitoring hours for the assigned project, but it is crucial also to track the rest of the hours.

Through this, you will be able to realize the unproductive things you always do and then focus on how to improve on them. For example, you may be wasting your time chatting, going through social media platforms, or web browsing.

Also, tracking each and every hour will allow you to identify hours for doing crucial things. Some of the top-notch things to do during these hours include cooking homemade meals, interacting with your family, and getting to the gym.

Therefore, starting tracking all your time today so that you can become more productive and successful.

7. Create A Boundary Between 'Home' Space And 'Work' Space

Most people prefer homeworking because it allows you to work from any place. Also, most individuals working from home typically make movements only to their living rooms, kitchen tables, and to their home offices. Some do all these and then end up becoming more productive and successful.

Just like you can walk into the company's office from one day to another, there is also a mindset shift when your home office featuring your desk, computers, and other essential supplies.

This shift plays a crucial role by doing something great for the home-based worker's brain. Also, this shift helps in designating to the home-based worker's family that they are following their day to day work schedule. Thus, this means you will not get disturbed by the family members.

8. Decluttering The Physical Space
A tidy workspace must be your primary area of focus. It plays a crucial role in ensuring you don't get disturbed by the junk surrounding you. Other than this, a tidy workplace helps a lot in saving your time and money.

In general, a company is likely to lose around 2.5 US million dollars because of a lack of organization. Research shows that this loss will happen because of a lack of productivity, and this results from distractions.

Other than this, a messy desk increases the chances of viruses to linger on germy smartphones or keyboards. This issue is likely to result in more sick days if it happens.
Therefore, it is crucial to set aside some time at least once per week to clean your workspace. You only need up to ten minutes to do this.

9. Purchase Ergonomic and Comfortable Furniture To Use In Your Office
Sitting on that office chair for more than eight hours per day is not something recommendable. But you don't have an otherwise. You need to face it if what you do demands a computer and sitting the whole day.

It's recommended to go for a standing desk or improvise with a counter or high table. Also, you need to take frequent breaks where you stand up and have short walks. Other than this, it is crucial to have walking meetings or walking calls.

Also, it is good to buy office furniture that supports good posture. Other than this, you need to fit it correctly for the body's ergonomics.

10. The Right Ambiance

Offices spaces are referred to as being controversial because each employee works differently. Also, when working from your home, it is crucial to come up with this kind of environment. Here, you need to light the perfect candle, have a clean desk, find the right playlist, and many more.

If you're an introvert individual or someone who finds it hard to work in a noisy environment, it is good to work in a tranquil atmosphere. Avoid coffee shops or open office since these are likely to distract you as your work.

However, not all individuals are equal. Some will work comfortably while listening to videos on YouTube, watching a TV, and playing online applications. But, don't try these if you cannot manage.
It is crucial to find something that works excellently for you so that the ambiance can get you in the groove of the work.

11. Avoid Social Media

Research shows that most individuals waste more than two hours per single day on various social media platforms. Yes, it is not wrong to do so, but this ends up making most workers less productive, which affects the company at the end of the day. Most individuals are the worst when it comes to wasting time on various social media platforms. Most will get on Facebook or Twitter to see new updates, but they end up spending up to an hour

answering other people's questions or responding
to some posts.

Social media platforms are the best for anyone
working from home since they can feel lonely.
Also, when working from your home office, you
will have enough to escape and interact with your
friends online. However, you need to be careful
since social media can end up sweeping away the
time you need to work.
As a home-based worker, you need to set timers
using extensions and applications so that you can
stay on track and avoid screenshots of social media
URLs while working.

12. Check Emails At Specific Times

Another thing that is likely to waste much of your
time is checking emails. Also, you can't work
comfortably if your inbox keeps sending
notifications of new emails.
A more productive and successful home-based
worker is not always on is not always connected
and is not available at all times. Therefore, this is
the path to follow if you want to become more
productive and earn more.

Always have a specific time when you will be
checking all your emails. Also, you need to ensure
that notifications are off so that you don't keep
getting disturbed whenever an individual sends an
email.

Sometimes it is good to set something like an auto-
responder that reminds you not to allow
distractions to control you. For example, you can
respond to your emails at specific time intervals
like 10 a.m, 2 p.m, and 5 p.m.

13. Set Expectations About Working Time

One hardest thing associated with homeworking is managing indicators or expectations with the housemates and family members.

For example, your partner may always like to discuss in detail their day whenever they get home. But this is likely to distract you if you're still working on your daily project.

In this case, you need to set expectations and indicators relating to off time and work time so you can always be happy and not ignored or interrupted. Thus, this explains the importance of the work schedule and setting a specific time to quit your job.

For example, you can decide to keep your family members updated that you're busy using lights. Here, you can turn the lights on when you're working or on calls so that you can avoid interruptions.

14. Productive Ways For Procrastinating

You're likely to do more work if you allow your mind to relax and refresh. However, sometimes we end up wasting much of our time because of using unproductive ways to procrastinate.

Sometimes you will plan to do something constructive within a short period but end up doing the opposite. For example, you can decide to watch a 5-minute YouTube Video on how to arrange your home office, but end up watching a different 20-minute video on the best places to visit in the world.

Therefore, consider coming up with productive ways of procrastinating that help you in achieving your short-term and long-term goals.

For some individuals, when they have a break, they will go to their kitchens and do some fun

things like cooking. Others will have a short walk
within their houses. Also, others utilize this time in
coming up with an outline for a specific article.
It is crucial to give your mind as you work.
However, you need to take care not to waste those
breaks.

15. As For Help If You're A Parent

Working from your home means facing a unique
challenge if you're a parent. You're likely to take
yourself as being less productive if you work while
taking care of your kids at the same time.
Just like any office work, it is crucial to work
comfortably without getting interrupted with your
children for the specified time. Taking care of your
younger ones and working from home at the same
is not as easy as you may think. For some people,
they expect parents to work and take care of their
children at the same time. However, it is not easy
to balance this when working from your home
office.

In this case, you need to ask for help so that you
can manage to complete your daily tasks as you
work from home. For some parents, they
accomplish this issue by ensuring one that one
works at late hours, and the other one works at the
early hours.
For other families, they find it enjoyable to take
their children to part-time daycare facilities so that
they can work comfortably without any
interruptions.

It is crucial to address your employer if you find
the above ways not to be working. When you do
this, the employer will come in and help you in
finding the most appropriate for this issue.

16. Turn Off Notifications

Notifications are the primary sources of distractions when it comes to homeworking. They are addictive and irresistible features, meaning we need to do everything to ensure they are off. Some examples of these notifications include Slack, Facebook, YouTube, Twitter, and many more. The current world is full of applications that always want to remove your attention from your daily schedule. For you to be productive and more successful, you need to turn off all these app notifications whenever working and check them only during your breaks. Never give yourself a chance to waste time because of notices.

17. Use The Most Appropriate Tools To Remain On Track

For entrepreneurs or freelancers, it is crucial to invest in the tools capable of making your work easier.

Other than investing in trade-specific tools, it is crucial to invest in inexpensive ways for your automation tasks so that you don't request for help to complete this.

For example, you can use Calendly, which is a tool linked with Google Calendar, when it comes to scheduling your calls. Whenever the person you've assigned the work completes the form, they will receive an email plus a link to schedule the most appropriate time for chatting on the calendar.

Other than this, with Calendly, you will have the opportunity to keep your productivity high since you will only schedule your calls on specific days. You have the option of automating different things such as invoicing, proposals, project management, and many more.

18. Noise-Canceling Headphones

It is excellent when you work without getting interfered with audio distractions.

Thus, this is the point why you need the services offered by noise-canceling headphones. You need these while working from your home office, while in airports or while on phone calls.

Also, with noise-canceling headphones, you will minimize distractions as you work so that you can focus on your day to day project.

19. Online Community

One primary disadvantage associated with homeworking is missing the in-person community or in-person co-workers.

Yes, dogs and cats can be your great work buddies, but they don't guarantee the stimulating discussions that allow you to get over humps as you work, create new tests and think of other excellent ideas.

With online communities, you will get the right solution to the lack of in-person element. Here, you will have access to a wide range of online communities such as Slack communities, LinkedIn communities, Facebook communities, and Twitter communities. With these communities, you will get an easy time when it comes to asking questions, sharing wins, complaining, laughing, and many more.

So, it is crucial to identify online communities that work excellently for you. Through this, you will remain in the right look and feel like other crews.

20. Leave Your House

Working from any place is one great benefit associated with homeworking. For example, you can decide to work from coffee shops where you only need to buy a snack or drink.

Also, you can decide to work from a co-working space. Another excellent option is to go to your friend's house and work from there. Furthermore, you can choose to complete your day to day tasks outside on one of the restaurant patios whenever the weather is okay.

Changing working places play a crucial role in inspiring new ideas. Also, changing workplaces is the best thing to do since it ensures you're more productive by igniting your motivation.

21. Keep Friends And Family Members Informed About Your Work

Homeworking can make you feel lonely in the cases where you slog the work out by yourself. When you keep your family informed about what you do, they will know how crucial the work and avoid interrupting you. Also, this helps a lot in giving your family investment in what you're doing.

When your family and friends understand what you do, you will get more motivated and hence, more productive.

22. Break The Routine At Least Once In A While

Yes, it is crucial to create a work routine. But it is also critical to break it up at least once in a while. For example, you can decide to take your cat to one of the nearest parks in the afternoon. Also, you can choose to attend the morning or evening coffee networking meeting.

Other than this, you can set aside some hours of midday and visit a local art museum. The flexibility of work schedules is one outstanding benefit associated with homeworking. When you

break the routine at least once in a while, you will
increase your chances of becoming more
productive and successful.

23. 20-20-20 Rule

With this 20-20-20 rule, you will get an easy way
of preventing eye strain, a condition that happens
when you stare at your computer screen for several
hours per day.
In this case, you need to give yourself a 20-second
off after staring at your computer for 20 minutes.

You need to utilize your break by focusing on a
particular object located twenty feet away. By
doing this, you will end up relaxing the muscles of
your eyes.
When you use blue-light blocking glasses or try
this rule, you will get an easy way of keeping your
eyes healthy at all times.

Conclusion

When you're realistic about work from home pros and cons, this type of working will be more profitable, exciting, and even empowering. With home working, you will get an easy way of escaping the day to day grind. It is the perfect option for you without considering if you're a full-time employee, part-timer employee, or freelancer.

However, you must be ready to face the many more responsibilities that come because of the freedom offered by work from home. Other added responsibilities include focus, planning, self-discipline, and foresight. Also, be ready to get interrupted several hours as you work hard to meet your daily schedule.

Be ready to come across individuals who don't categorize working from home as a form of employment. Be prepared to work during the nights and over the weekends because you messed up with your deadlines. In general, and as per the majority of the home-based employees, working from home is not as easy as you may think - it is only a different workplace.

References

https://blog.hubspot.com/marketing/work-from-home-jobs

https://www.flexjobs.com/blog/post/top-companies-work-from-anywhere-remote-jobs/

https://blog.hubspot.com/marketing/productivity-tips-working-from-home

https://www.businessnewsdaily.com/5731-top-companies-for-telecommuting-jobs.html

https://www.inc.com/christina-desmarais/get-more-done-18-tips-for-telecommuters.html

https://www.thebalancecareers.com/top-telecommuting-companies-3542783

https://open.buffer.com/remote-work/

https://blog.hubstaff.com/disadvantages-of-working-from-home/

https://kinsta.com/blog/working-remotely/

https://clark.com/employment-military/work-home-guide/

https://pingboard.com/work-life-balance/

www.ingramcontent.com/pod-product-compliance
Lightning Source LLC
Chambersburg PA
CBHW051135250726
48655CB00007B/3077